Symbols of Freedom

The Lincoln Memorial

Tristan Boyer Binns

Heinemann Library
Chicago, Illinois

Customer Service 888-454-2279

Visit our website at www.heinemannlibrary.com

Designed by Lisa Buckley
Printed in Hong Kong

05 04 03 02 01
10 9 8 7 6 5 4 3 2

Library of Congress Cataloging-in-Publication Data
Binns, Tristan Boyer, 1968-
  The Lincoln Memorial / Tristan Boyer Binns.
    p. cm. -- (Symbols of freedom)
  Includes bibliographical references (p.) and index.
  ISBN 1-58810-120-7 (lib. bdg.)   ISBN 1-58810-404-4 (pbk bdg.)
  1. Lincoln Memorial (Washington, D.C.) --Juvenile literature. 2. Lincoln, Abraham,
1809-1865--Monuments--Washington (D.C.)--Juvenile literature. 3. Washington
(D.C.)--Buildings, structures, etc.--Juvenile literature. [1. Lincoln Memorial
(Washington, D.C.) 2. National monuments.] I. Title.

F203.4.L73 B56 2001
973.7'092--dc21   00-058143

Acknowledgments
The author and publishers are grateful to the following for permission to reproduce copyright material: p.5 The Purcell Team/Corbis, p.6 Patrick Ward/Corbis, p.8 Chris Rodgers/Rainbow/PictureQuest, p.9 Reuters NewMedia Inc./Corbis, p.10 Thomas Fletcher/Stock, Boston/PictureQuest, p.11 William Weems/Woodfin Camp/PictureQuest, p.12 Jay Syverson/Corbis, p.13 Thomas McAvoy/TimePix, p.14 Dennis Brack/Black Star Publishing/PictureQuest, p.15, 16, 21, 23, 27 Bettemann/Corbis, p.17 Hulton-Deutsch Collection/Corbis, p.18, 19, 22, 25, 26, 28 Corbis, p.20 National Archives, p.24 Chicago Historical Society, p.29 Library of Congress.
Cover photograph by Ron Watts/Corbis.

Every effort has been made to contact copyright holders of any material reproduced in this book. Any omissions will be rectified in subsequent printings if notice is given to the publisher.

Some words are shown in bold, **like this.**
You can find out what they mean by looking in the glossary.

Contents

What Is the Lincoln Memorial?

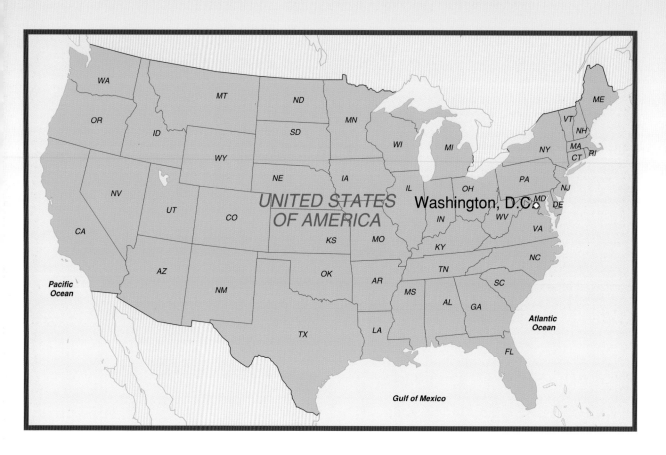

The Lincoln Memorial is a famous building. It is in a park in Washington, D.C., the **capital** of the United **States.**

The Lincoln Memorial is a **symbol** of the **union** between all of the 50 states. It stands for the freedom we enjoy as Americans. It reminds us that we must work together to keep our freedom.

What Are Memorials?

Memorials help people remember a person or an idea. A memorial can be a statue or a building. The Lincoln Memorial was built to **honor** President Abraham Lincoln.

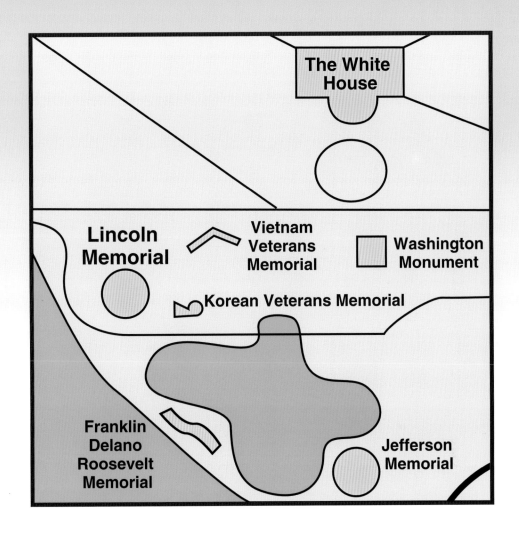

There are many memorials in Washington, D.C. Some honor presidents or other leaders. There are also memorials for people who fought in wars.

All Around You

Pictures of the Lincoln Memorial are all around you. More than 80 million pennies show the Lincoln Memorial on the back. President Lincoln's face is on the front.

The Lincoln Memorial is also shown on the back of every five-dollar bill. President Lincoln's face is on the front, too.

Outside the Lincoln Memorial

The Lincoln Memorial is made of white **marble.**
It has a big porch with rows of **columns.**
There are 56 steps that lead up to it.

The Lincoln Memorial is at the edge of a long pool of water. People can look into the water and see a **reflection** of the building.

What Is Inside?

Inside, there is one big room and two smaller rooms. A giant statue of Abraham Lincoln is in the big room. He looks serious but kind.

RATHER TO BE DEDICATED HERE TO
THE UNFINISHED WORK WHICH THEY
WHO FOUGHT HERE HAVE THUS FAR
SO NOBLY ADVANCED · IT IS RATHER FOR
US TO BE HERE DEDICATED TO THE
GREAT TASK REMAINING BEFORE US-
THAT FROM THESE HONORED DEAD
WE TAKE INCREASED DEVOTION TO
THAT CAUSE FOR WHICH THEY GAVE THE
LAST FULL MEASURE OF DEVOTION -
THAT WE HERE HIGHLY RESOLVE THAT
THESE DEAD SHALL NOT HAVE DIED IN
VAIN - THAT THIS NATION UNDER GOD
SHALL HAVE A NEW BIRTH OF FREEDOM-
AND THAT GOVERNMENT OF THE PEOPLE
BY THE PEOPLE FOR THE PEOPLE SHALL
NOT PERISH FROM THE EARTH·

Each of the small rooms has an important speech carved into a wall. Above the speeches are **murals.** They are about freedom and **union.**

13

Meeting at the Lincoln Memorial

For years, the Lincoln Memorial has been a meeting place for people. Large crowds sometimes gather there. Often, they do this to show others how they feel about something.

On Lincoln's birthday each year, the president lays a **wreath** at the Lincoln Memorial. Leaders from other countries often go there to show their respect.

A Place for Equal Rights

Marian Anderson was a famous opera singer. She was African American. In 1939, she was not allowed to sing in one concert hall in Washington, D.C. So she sang outside the Lincoln Memorial instead.

In the 1960s, Dr. Martin Luther King, Jr.,
gave a famous speech in front of the
Lincoln Memorial. The speech was about
his dream of equal rights for all people.

President Abraham Lincoln

Abraham Lincoln was president during the 1860s. Some **states** in our country argued over **slavery.** Then the northern states fought the southern states in the **Civil War.**

18

When the Civil War ended, Lincoln was killed.
He had helped free the slaves and bring the
United States back together. But the man who
shot Lincoln hated him for those things.

Remembering Lincoln

After Abraham Lincoln died, people wanted to build a memorial to him. It took almost 50 years before it was built. There were many different ideas about how it should look.

Everyone decided that the memorial should look like a **temple** from ancient Greece. It would be in a park. There would be a statue of Lincoln inside.

21

Building the Memorial

The **cornerstone** for the Lincoln Memorial was laid on February 15, 1915. It would take seven more years to finish the building.

It was a lot of work. The park had been a swamp. There had to be a lot of **concrete** under the ground to hold up the heavy **marble.**

A Huge Statue

After the building began, Daniel Chester French was chosen to make the statue of Abraham Lincoln. At first, he wanted to make the statue about as tall as one basketball goal.

24

Then French went to the building. He saw that the statue would have to be bigger. So he made it as tall as three basketball goals on top of each other!

Almost Real

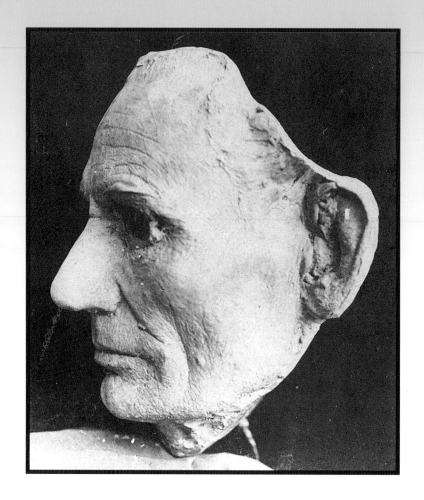

French used real **castings** of Abraham Lincoln's face and hands to make the sculpture. The face even shows Lincoln's **mole!**

26

The statue of Lincoln was made in New York. It was sent to Washington, D.C. in 28 pieces. They fit together just like a jigsaw puzzle.

Great Celebration

On May 30, 1922, more than 50,000 people met at the new Lincoln Memorial. They were there for its **dedication.** Men who had fought in the **Civil War** sat in the front row.

A man spoke about what Lincoln had meant to
African Americans. He was Dr. Robert Moton, an
African American writer and teacher. From then
on, the Lincoln Memorial was a **symbol** of **unity.**

29

Fact File

Lincoln Memorial statue

★ The statue weighs as much as 24 school buses.

★ Lincoln's thumb is the size of a football.

★ His head is as big as an armchair.

★ A man could walk under Lincoln's leg without hitting his head.

★ The statue is made of white Georgia **marble.**

★ There are only 48 states listed on the outside of the Lincoln Memorial. That is because there were only 48 states when it was built!

Glossary

capital important city where the government is located

casting part of a statue made by putting a type of plaster over part of a person's body, then taking it off and filling the shape with a liquid that hardens and looks exactly like the person

Civil War U.S. war in the 1800s, in which northern states fought against southern states

column tall, round post that holds up the roof or other part of a building

concrete kind of man-made stone

cornerstone first stone of a building that is going to be built

dedication ceremony in which a place is opened to the public

honor to do something that shows great respect for someone or something

marble hard, white stone used to make buildings and statues

mole small, raised spot on the skin

mural large painting on walls

reflection image that bounces off a flat, smooth surface such as a mirror or water

slavery practice of owning human beings to do work

state group of people joined together under one government

symbol something that stands for an idea

temple building where people worshiped their gods in ancient times

union strength of all the parts of the United States of America working together as one country

unity ability of people of all races and beliefs to live and work together

wreath ring of flowers placed on a grave or important place as a sign of respect

More Books to Read

Goldstein, Ernest. *The Statue Abraham Lincoln.* Minneapolis, Minn.: Lerner Publishing Group, 1997.

Kent, Deborah. *The Lincoln Memorial.* Danbury, Conn.: Children's Press, 1996. An older reader can help you with this book.

Schafer, Lola M. *Abraham Lincoln.* Mankato, Minn.: Capstone Press, 1999.

Index